# POTTED
## AND
# PRUNED

Diana,

Happy Gardening!

*[signature]*

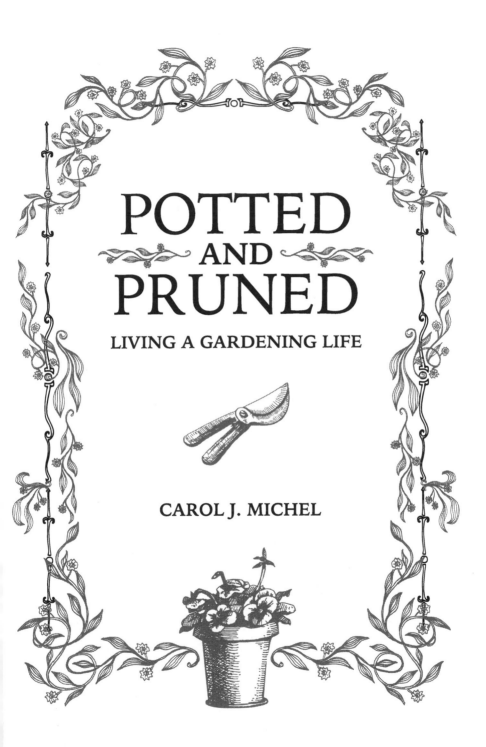

# POTTED
## AND
# PRUNED

## LIVING A GARDENING LIFE

### CAROL J. MICHEL

Gardenangelist Books

Editor: Deb Wiley
Managing Editor: Katie Elzer-Peters
Copy Editor: Billie Brownell
Designer: Nathan Bauer

ISBN-10: 0-9986979-1-5
ISBN-13: 978-0-9986979-1-8

Printed in the United States of America

For Mom, who never called me out of the garden, and for Dad, who never shooed me out of the garden.

# Contents

# CHAPTER 1

# YES, I AM AN ECCENTRIC GARDENER

On one of those rare occasions when my siblings and I were gathered together as adults around the dinner table at my parents' house, my older sister proclaimed to everyone there that I was the most likely of the five of us to become an eccentric later in life. Her reason? Because I was the one who gardened.

Eccentric and gardener. The two go hand in hand, or hand in gardening glove, don't they? Some people think so, probably because we provide considerable evidence when we are out in our gardens in our best gardening outfits—which, for me, almost always includes a green T-shirt—planting, pruning, potting up, and performing what others might assume to be secret rituals learned from other gardeners. We are lost in our gardens and rarely realize the spectacle we sometimes become as we lean down to sniff a flower or snip a bloom, exposing our broad side for the entire world to see.

There are countless stories and legends to back up this notion that eccentricity and gardening go together, and I'm not just talking about tales of my own gardening adventures. There are numerous stories found in books and articles. I remember browsing for hours on end—even in my pre-teen years—through the 1961 edition of *How to Grow Vegetables & Fruits by the Organic Method* edited by J. I. Rodale. If the copy I checked out over and over again from the local public library when I was a kid still exists with the lending card in the pocket on the inside cover, I'm sure my name would be on it more than anyone else's. Later in life, I purchased my own "good used copy" which makes for pleasant reading on cold winter days. I've even purchased copies and given them to other gardeners I thought worthy of this book. It was in *How to Grow Vegetables & Fruits by the Organic Method* that I first came across the story of Mrs. H. R. Leversee of Kalamazoo, Michigan, who was quoted as saying, "I like to work with plain dirt." Don't all gardeners?

According to the story, which must have taken place in the early 1940s, Mrs. Leversee set out nearly every day with her wheelbarrow and shovel and walked up and down her street scooping up the dirt that "lines the gutters." They estimated she transported 100 tons of soil from the street to her garden over the course of 17 years, and she wore out three wheelbarrows. No doubt she also wore down numerous shovels along the way. I bet her neighbors wondered what she was doing out there nearly every day of the year, year after year, walking around with her wheelbarrow and shovel, scooping up dirt. After the first several years, hopefully they got used to the sight of Mrs. Leversee with her wheelbarrow and realized she was just a gardener, one who loved her garden. She was quoted as saying, "Working is like walking. If you enjoy it you never notice it. I like to work with plain dirt. I like to see things grow in it. Every shovelful I take from along the curbs will produce food some day. I'll never get tired of watching that happen."

What a great attitude to have about gardening. Yes, gardening sometimes looks like work and feels like work. And at the end of a day in our gardens many of us feel quite worked over. But the result, whether it is flowers, vegetables, or even a nicely manicured lawn and landscape, is our reward. We never grow tired of the rewards even if it means the neighbors think of us as a bit odd, even eccentric.

I thought later about what my sister proclaimed that evening at dinner and decided to look up "eccentric" in the dictionary. I chose an online dictionary (*freedictionary. com*) that included illustrations, presumably to make the definitions more clear. They defined "eccentric" as a "person with an unusual or odd personality" and next to that definition they showed a caricature of what they considered an eccentric—a person with a funny hat and an arm full of flowers, standing beside a watering can.

I guess my sister was right. I was the gardener; therefore, I would be the family eccentric. I embraced it. I strive now to be the best eccentric gardener I can be, working in my garden, thinking about gardens, and writing about gardening. I also call myself a gardenangelist, an evangelist for gardening, ready to encourage others to garden too.

For over twelve years, I've published many of my

thoughts and ideas on gardening on a blog I call *May Dreams Gardens (maydreamsgardens.com)* because all year I dream of the days of May when the sun is warm, the sky is blue, the grass is green, and the garden is new again. The winter is past and an entire growing season is before me. It's one of my favorite times of the year.

Now I've potted up and pruned many of my favorite thoughts and ideas on gardening from my blog for this book of essays. I hope those who read them find some useful seeds of wisdom, a few kernels of encouragement, and some new ways to become their own kind of gardener, their own brand of eccentric, perhaps even a gardenangelist, as they work on whatever plot of land they feel called to garden on.

CHAPTER 2

# WHAT'S IN A NAME?

Do you know the difference between your garden and the garden of someone who is rich?

There are obvious differences because of what money can buy. Money can buy land measured in acres, exotic plants from around the world, full-time landscape and gardening crews, great designs by the best landscape architects, one-of-a-kind garden art, and dazzling water features.

But the real difference between your garden and the gardens of those who are rich is that rich people *name* their gardens.

Technically, rich people name their entire estates, which include the mansions or castles or manor houses plus the surrounding gardens. We identify these estate names as the names of great gardens. We read about gardens like Great Dixter, Sissinghurst, and Hidcote in Great Britain, to name just a few. Rich people in the United States name their estates too. Who has been to Winterthur, Oldfields, or Blithewold, all estate gardens of people who had money and named their gardens?

I've had three gardens so far, and I'll admit that the one I garden in now is the only garden I named. It never occurred to me to name my first two gardens. Then as I read about more of the great named gardens, I decided that perhaps I could give my garden a bit of grandeur by giving it a name, even though it sits on a mere one-third of an acre with a house in the middle of it.

My experience, and that of fellow gardeners, is you shouldn't expect to pick a name on the first day you stand in your new garden. You should first spend time in the garden, getting to know it–even over several seasons–and then a good name will pop into your head. I thought about the name of my garden for quite some time before it came to me one day in May.

Every year, for as long as I worked, I took off a week or longer in May to spend time planting the vegetable garden and opening up the entire garden for the season. All year I dreamed of those upcoming days of May, so I decided to call my garden "May Dreams Gardens."

If you think it's pretentious to name your garden, consider the amount of time, sweat, and money you are putting into it. Doesn't that alone make it worthy of a name?

But I didn't stop at naming my garden. Once I had a proper garden design, I began to name all the different borders and beds throughout my grand one-third-acre estate. Names made it easier to write about my garden and reminded me what the focus of each border and bed was supposed to be.

In The Garden of Southern Follies and Delights, I am

attempting to grow camellias and other Southern plants that most people don't attempt to grow as far north as where I live. Trying to grow these plants will prove to be either my folly or my delight. They are my delight when I imagine them softly humming "Dixie" as I weed around them and marvel at the symmetry of a camellia bloom. They are my folly as I do my best each fall to provide suitable and necessary protection for them and hope again for a mild winter.

Across the way—and by way I mean about five feet—from The Garden of Southern Follies and Delights is a perennial border I affectionately call Plopper's Field. In Plopper's Field, which is not much bigger than 10 feet by 10 feet, I plop perennials in wherever there seems to be a bare spot of ground and it appears that the plant I am planting won't be taller than the one behind it. Of course, over the years I've misjudged more than a few plants' abilities to grow tall and so one day I intend to dig up everything in Plopper's Field and replant it. By the way, "one day" is the code phrase that means I probably won't get around to it, unless one day a grave plant disease or a wild herd of meadow voles wipes out the entire border. I shudder at the thought.

Next to Plopper's Field and behind a large spruce tree is The Shrubbery, where I planted flowering shrubs and placed a few chairs just in case I should grow tired while gardening and want to sit down. With mostly shrubs, it's an easy border to take care of compared to Plopper's Field, where some flower always needs to be deadheaded. But I wasn't completely successful in avoiding perennials in

The Shrubbery. I planted some lavender near the chairs just to have something to smell should I grow tired and decide to sit down.

Across the back of the entire garden, which sounds richer than saying "across the back of the entire backyard," is The Vegetable Garden Cathedral, with six raised beds for growing vegetables and annual flowers. Occasionally, The Vegetable Garden Cathedral is also home to a few plants that need a place to grow a bit before being moved on to another part of the garden.

Why call it The Vegetable Garden Cathedral? The rows of raised beds where I grow vegetables remind me of the rows of pews in a church, and I often spend Sunday mornings tending them. It is also the center of activity in my garden, much as the church was once the center of activity in a village.

On the opposite side of the lawn from The Shrubbery are two large borders divided by a path. I call the path Ridgewood Avenue, the name of the street where one of my favorite garden writers from the twentieth century, the Southern garden writer and designer Elizabeth Lawrence, lived. On one side of Ridgewood Avenue is Woodland Follies, where a redbud tree once provided shade for a few rescued woodland plants. Then the redbud fell over one hot day during the middle of the worst drought we have ever had, and the woodland plants ended up in full sun. I've since planted trees to replace the redbud and provide shade once again, but they are taking their time so it is still a folly to grow shade-loving plants there, but I continue to try.

On the other side of Ridgewood Avenue is another border called August Dreams Gardens. I try to remember to only plant late-blooming flowers in this mostly native prairie-style garden. I sometimes forget, but most of the time I stick with the plan and by late summer, August Dreams Gardens becomes the focal point of the entire back garden.

Near the patio is a large honeylocust tree surrounded by a circular border planted with low-growing, shade-tolerant flowers in palettes of mostly pinks and whites. I call this border Bird's Blanket, not because birds lay there and sleep, but because there are a couple of bird feeders perched near the edge that I sometimes remember to fill with seeds, especially in the wintertime.

On the street side of the house, I call the entire front garden Neighbor's View to remind me that this is the garden the neighbors see. I try to keep from planting it to look like a crazy gardening lady lives here. I'm not sure how good a job I've done with that theme, but then again, maybe that's what it should look like.

I just recently decided on names for the side gardens, areas I don't really focus on but probably should as they provide the routes to the gates to the back garden. Neither side is much more than miscellaneous plants I've tossed in over the years so I decided to call them "muddles." The west side is now called Lilac Muddle, in honor of three large lilacs that always seem to need a good pruning. The east side is now called Ginkgo Muddle to honor the ginkgo tree I planted there several years ago, hoping in time for a glorious display of golden fall color.

I still have some garden areas without names. I'm patient. It's only been twenty years since I started gardening here. I'm sure names for the unnamed areas will reveal themselves in due time.

# CHAPTER 3

# A GARDEN IS A STORY TOLD BY PLANTS

A garden is a story told by plants.

When the time is right, the plants tell the stories: stories of the past and the present, stories of conquests and defeats, stories of friends and enemies. The only way to hear these stories is to go out to the garden, look around, and let the plants tell their tales in their own time.

I've heard many stories in my own garden, some worth telling to others and some that are best kept a secret between me and the plants. There are stories of obsessions, mostly my obsessions with one type of plant or another, at one time or another, like the Orienpet lilies standing tall above my perennial border, Plopper's Field. I hardly knew the lilies' names and hardly knew they existed before I first saw them in a nursery. I became obsessed with them on first sight, and I made a quick decision to plant as many as I could in my own garden.

Other plants tell stories of how they arrived in my garden. Some came as passalong plants, like 'Bath's Pink' dianthus. This particular dianthus started out as a bunch of roots and stems in a paper grocery bag left on my doorstep. The giver told me it would practically grow on concrete. She was right. I watched for several years as the dianthus nearly took over a two feet swath of the edge of my concrete patio before I interrupted its tale of conquest and banished it to a more suitable location where it could grow and take over as far as it liked.

The ditch lilies on the side of the house tell two stories, starting with their beginnings as a single passalong plant given to me by a well-meaning friend when I was desperate for any plants to grow in my new and bare suburban lot. So desperate was my need for plants that I abandoned good sense and planted that one ditch lily in an out-of-the-way side garden. I was sure I could contain that one plant. But its story grew, as did the ground it took over. Now when the ditch lilies bloom they remind me of the drive down country highways and roads toward the annual family reunion. Looking at the passing landscape from the backseat window, I saw ditch lilies in bloom along the roads and down the country lanes that led back to old farmhouses. Eventually, after what seemed like the entire day but was really only a few hours, we'd turn down one of those country lanes, the one that led to our grandparents' farm. Now the idea of completely getting rid of the ditch lilies in my garden, as much of a nuisance as they are, seems to me like getting rid of a cherished family memory. So I keep them and contain them as best I can.

Out in my vegetable garden, The Vegetable Garden Cathedral, the plants tell more family stories. They tell stories of gardens I knew long ago, where tomatoes grew to eight feet and taller. Where running up and down the rows of my Dad's vegetable garden was like running through a jungle, one of squash, beans, peppers, and tomatoes. The vegetable garden also tells stories of family gatherings where okra and eggplant picked that same day were then battered and fried and served at suppertime. When I'm out in my vegetable garden, I still hear the congenial arguments among my uncles about whether tomatoes should be sugared or salted. I settle the argument by eating my tomatoes plain.

Sometimes, plants with injured leaves tell tales of insect invasions or diseases that seem to come like thieves in the night into the garden. Late in summer, many plants also tell tales of hot summer days and pop-up thunderstorms amid the twinkling lights of fireflies.

In one of my gardens, the plants tell tales of the South and wonder how they ended up so far north. I can almost hear the opening song of the movie *"Gone With The Wind"* when the camellias tell their stories. When they bloom, it is a time to rejoice.

Occasionally, the plants speak only in soft whispers. You have to stop gardening and pause for a bit to hear them. Other days they all try to tell their stories at the same time, like a band trying to play without a conductor. They tell stories I enjoy hearing year after year and they surprise me with new stories I hope to pass on to others.

Every plant has its own story to tell, and collectively they are the story of my garden, the story of my life.

CHAPTER 4

## ALL GARDENERS ARE DELUSIONAL

I do my best thinking on my knees in my garden, perhaps with my head stuck under the grape arbor pulling out all manner of thistles, grasses, pokeweeds, mulberry tree seedlings, and redbud tree seedlings. The redbud seedlings are especially prolific in my garden even though the redbud has been gone for several years.

One hot, sultry, windless summer day, the redbud, which offered the only shade suitable for some rescued woodland plants, inexplicably fell over when I was hundreds of miles away, about to wet my toes in the Atlantic Ocean. I had just texted news of my arrival to my sister, who was caring for my garden in the middle of what turned out to be the driest summer we'd ever had, when she texted back, "Did you know your redbud fell over?"

After my sister texted me the news with a picture for evidence, I quickly rounded up a crew to come in and clear out the tree, leaving all those rescued woodland plants exposed to full sun. Rather than sensibly moving them to another area with shade, I just kept watering them and later that fall planted a little sour gum tree to eventually provide them with shade.

Now, every time I weed out redbud seedlings—and I have pulled out countless seedlings even four years after the mother tree died—I wonder if somehow the mother tree passed along a message to her seeds, some powerful instructions to germinate and grow as quickly as possible because the mother tree knew she was dying and would one day, on a hot, sultry, windless day in the middle of a drought, just fall over. The mother tree must have known she needed replacements and gave her seeds the power to last for years in my garden, germinating in waves year after year.

It was while kneeling under the grape arbor one evening cutting out a redbud seedling that had escaped my attention and was nearly tree sized that I had this thought and a revelation about weeds and gardeners. I realized all gardeners are delusional, and that is why year after year, season after season, we continue to hope and believe, in spite of evidence to the contrary, that if we just keep pulling out weeds and cutting back unwanted redbud and mulberry seedlings they will all get the message and leave our gardens alone.

So why isn't the message to stay out of our gardens embedded in the weed seeds' DNA? I would love that message to be, "Don't bother growing within this fenced in area. The gardener will find you and pull you out. Get out beyond the fence or forget about it." But that has not yet happened, or if it has happened, the weed seeds in my garden are ignoring the message.

So I continue to pull weeds.

I rarely get all the roots, but when I think I have, I raise the weed with its fully intact roots up over my head with a triumphant fist pump to commemorate my victory, then throw it unceremoniously into a tub, and move on. There's a weed that will never sully my garden again!

Sometimes, though, when I am most delusional, I simply keep cutting back the weeds, weeds like nutsedge and dandelions. I use my weed whacker, intent on wearing the weeds out, knowing that the clean look of the garden after cutting back the weeds is just an illusion. The nutsedge will grow back again in a few days' time. The dandelions will likewise recover and use their giant taproots to grow new crowns of leaves. I bury purslane with a sharp swipe of my hoe, even though I know it will just root again and spring up even healthier and thicker than before. Of course, I know purslane is edible, as are dandelions, but I refuse to eat the enemies of my garden. I cannot bring myself to welcome them as guests to my dinner table, even in a salad bowl or on a dinner plate. Can you really trust your enemies?

If the definition of delusional is knowing something is true but then ignoring that truth and coming up with one's own version of what is true, then I am guilty of such in my garden when I think about weeds. But if I or any gardener was other than delusional when it comes to weeds, if we did not believe we could win the battle against them, then we would have long ago thrown down our dandelion diggers, yanked off our gardening gloves, and gone inside, out of the sun and humidity, away from the mosquitoes and ticks, and taken up some other hobby like painting china plates.

Yet we aren't painting china plates. We are still weeding. We are still gardening. The reason? I can only think it is because we must be delusional, or we would never garden at all.

# CHAPTER 5

# GARDEN CARETAKERS, GARDEN HEROES

I start off every gardening season intent on being a good caretaker for my garden. After a long winter of rest, I go out in early spring with great plans and high hopes.

I plan to deadhead blooms long before they cast their seeds about the garden. I envision effortless hours spent spreading the finest mulch on each flower border and along the paths of the vegetable garden so everything looks orderly and well kept, as though a wonderful, attentive caregiver tends the garden. When I am the caretaker, I pull out weeds when they are small and dainty and willingly let loose from the soil with just the slightest tug. That is, if there are even any weeds at all after the fine job I will have done with mulching.

When I am the caretaker of my garden, all the plants will naturally have water when they need it, which will fall gently from the heavens onto the garden precisely when the garden needs it, usually after midnight and before 4 a.m. Of course, I stand at the ready to provide water with a garden hose that never kinks.

No plants on my fantasy garden caretaking watch ever wither and die without a good reason. Diseases and insects stop just on the other side of the fence and admire the garden from afar, side by side with the rabbits, raccoons, and meadow voles. They dare not enter my well-cared-for garden.

Who wouldn't want to be the garden caretaker I imagine myself to be?

Then, on the second day of the gardening season, I look about and realize there are some problems in the garden. I see weeds coming up and growing in all the garden beds. Perhaps my fall sweep through the garden to get those pesky weeds wasn't as thorough as I'd planned. I note the mulch is thin in some spots, and already the garden could use a good day or two, perhaps a week of my time to get it back into some sense of order.

It is then that I cast off my clean and carefully pressed "I Love to Garden" caretaker's apron and switch to the cape and tights of a garden hero.

In my new outfit I am in full garden hero mode. Captain HortHero to the rescue! I begin flinging mulch from one bed to another and hope by some miracle it will actually cause now full-grown weeds to wither and die while the plants I planted will flourish. Since this is rarely the case, I drag out a variety of weeding tools and begin the battle.

I proceed to cut back, pull out, hoe down, and otherwise exert all my energies on weeding.

Then I notice it hasn't rained for some time and plants are beginning to wilt, especially those languishing on the patio in the same containers in which they came home from the garden center weeks ago. I grab the hose that immediately senses my touch and kinks in three places, stubbornly refusing to deliver more than a trickle of water until I say the magic words and make offerings to the goddesses of the garden hoses in exchange for more water.

I've never quite figured out the magic words to unkink the hoses, so there I stand for what seems like hours but is probably just minutes, trickling water on each plant, hoping it is enough to revive them until I can slay the kinks of the garden hoses for good.

But there is no time just to be a hero with weeding and watering. I must valiantly deadhead, prune, tie up, and somehow get all the garden plants to behave, because by day two in the garden they are spewing seeds, growing in the wrong direction or not growing at all, and in some cases reaching out to attack one another.

I'm always a little surprised by the hooligan behavior of plants that looked so well-behaved in their pots at the garden center. Oh yes, many a plant has fooled me until I brought it home. Fooled or surprised, either way I am the hero rescuing one plant from another. I am also the disciplinarian, pulling plants apart, cutting off their seed heads, and otherwise using a variety of pruners and occasionally even saws to bring order out of the chaos created by my misbehaving plants.

And while I am scrambling around in full garden hero mode, with my cape flapping in the wind and my green tights tearing from the snags of the rose thorns, attacking weeds, pleading with the goddesses of the water hoses, and disciplining the misbehaving plants, the perimeter of my garden is breached. Countless insects, plant diseases, rabbits, raccoons, and meadow voles are coming in from all directions, ready to party in my garden and leave their messes for me to clean up.

Of course, I'm not invited to their parties nor told in advance when they are happening. They are like those midnight raves that just pop up. By morning, I can see the damage and add "clean up the mess made by fill-in-the-blank" to my ever-growing list of things to do as the garden hero who is going to save her garden and once again restore order and peace throughout the borders and beds.

It is the hope of order and peace in the garden, the dream of returning to the quiet life of a garden caretaker, that keeps me going from one day to the next, from one season to the next, year in and year out. I know I'll never be able to fully retire my garden hero cape and my torn green tights, but it would be nice to occasionally be able to rightfully wear the caretaker's "I Love to Garden" apron, to be caught up on weeding, watering, and plant disciplining, to just be a caretaker for awhile.

# CHAPTER 6

# FRASS

In college, I took two entomology classes. I took the first one because I was required to do so to earn the college degree I wanted. I took the second one because I enjoyed the first class and wanted to learn more about insects. Insects, as it turned out, were not as scary and creepy as I thought they'd be. They were really rather fascinating.

But in those two classes, no one ever mentioned the word "frass." I would have remembered such a word. Frass. I had to wait some 30 years or so to find out about frass. Ever since then I've been like a five-year-old who just learned a new word, a new cuss word.

Frass is the fancy word for insect poop. Once you know that word, the uses for it just boggle the mind.

"With all those cicadas in the trees, you should really wear a hat to avoid their frass dropping on your head."

"What is all this frass around the tomato plants? Hornworms, again!?"

"Oh, frass! I forgot to stop at the garden center."

Really, frass is a gardener's secret cuss word and has many uses. For example, imagine you walk out to the garden and find that rabbits have eaten all the green bean seedlings again. You can yell out, "Frass!" and no one will know you've just cussed.

Or when the neighbor kids are playing nearby and your garden hose kinks up on you again, you can freely say, "This hose is a real piece of frass!" Then the kids' parents won't get upset because you taught their kids a cuss word, even though, in a way, you did.

This is not a bunch of frass. It's a gardener's secret cuss word and one of the best new words I've learned in a long time.

# CHAPTER 7

## MY PHASES OF HOUSEPLANT CARE

I regularly cycle through four predictable phases caring for my houseplants.

In the first phase, *Acquire*, I buy the houseplant with promises to care for it and give it a spot where it will get the best light in the house. I vow to make sure it has a pretty pot to live in. I promise I will water it whenever it is thirsty and fertilize it when it shows even the first hint of a yellow leaf. I admire this wonderful plant I now have in my home and feel so happy to have it.

In the second phase, *Nurture*, I tend to follow through on most of my promises to the plant. I give it a good spot where there is plenty of light, water it when it is dry, and feed it at the first sign of a yellow leaf. I dust the leaves and mist the plant with distilled water while tenderly whispering to it sentiments such as, "Grow, little plant. Flower if you will. I love you."

In the third phase, *Neglect*, I begin to gradually fall short on my promise to take care of the plant. I let it go just a little longer between waterings and abandon the idea of fertilizer. I pull off the yellow leaves and wonder why the plant isn't doing well, if I notice it at all. I may even move it away from its spot in the best light because now it looks pale and limp. This phase often occurs in early to mid-spring when the outdoor gardening season is beginning. It can also occur just because I get busy or get lost in various rabbit holes found in books and on the internet and lose some of the time I would have normally spent caring for the plants.

In the fourth phrase, *Rescue*, I look at the plant one day and wonder how it got to be such a sorry-looking thing. I feel remorse. I feel horrible that I neglected the plant so much that it dropped nearly all of its leaves and its roots are tightly bound up in a pot that is two sizes too small. I immediately put on my Garden Hero cape and tights and begin a rescue operation. I cut off the dead leaves and stems and repot the plant in a larger pot with fresh potting soil. I return the plant to a spot where it will get the best light and begin again to regularly water and fertilize it. If it is summer, I might even take the plant outside for fresh air and better light. I dust its leaves and mist it while whispering, "I'm sorry, please grow again. I promise to be faithful to you and never let you dry out again."

I can and do repeat the cycles of Nurture, Neglect, and Rescue several times until at some point, the Rescue is too late. Then I quietly dispose of the plant, burying it in the compost bin, and start the entire cycle again with Acquire as soon as I see a pretty indoor plant that would look just perfect in the window where the other plant once grew.

## CHAPTER 8

# A LETTER TO MY FAVORITE T-SHIRT

*My dearest, oldest favorite gardening T-shirt,*

*I knew this day was coming. I could sense it when we last gardened together yesterday. This day when we would finally have to say goodbye to one another.*

*We had some good times in the garden, didn't we?*

*Remember all the times we planted the vegetable garden in May? You were as delighted as I was to feel the sun on your soft green fabric after months inside a dark drawer. I'll always appreciate, too, how willing you were to mow the lawn with me even though I'd sweat and get you all wet. You never complained. You were one of the best at keeping me cool.*

*I see now how all our time together in the garden has taken its toll on you, especially around your frayed and worn collar. Those holes on the shoulder seams too. Oh gosh, do you remember how you'd make those holes on your shoulders look like bugs and then I'd swat at them? I'd laugh and you'd, well, you did what T-shirts do when they play tricks on their wearer.*

*I've also noticed some stains on you that just won't go*

31

*away. I think these stains came from that time you helped me unload mulch from the bed of the pickup truck. It seems one corner of the truck's tailgate always had some grease on it that would get all over you.*

*I don't mind wearing you with some stains, not after all the seasons we've been through together in the garden. But lately, some holes have shown up in places where a lady might not want to have a hole in her T-shirt.*

*I know you are just worn out. I understand, truly. We had a good run, though, didn't we? How long has it been since you were crisp and new with a little price tag hanging from your collar? I'm guessing maybe 15 years? That's a long time for a T-shirt. You should be proud. I'm proud of you! You were my delight and always one of my all-time favorites.*

*Even though we won't be gardening together again, I'll never forget you. I'm going to keep you around. You deserve that. You don't deserve the rag drawer or, worse, the trash. No, you deserve to be kept all clean and nicely folded, in a place where we can meet every so often just to reminisce about how much less a bag of top soil seemed to weigh when we first gardened together.*

*As long as I'm around, you'll be around too. I promise.*

*Thank you, dearest T-shirt of mine, from the bottom of my gardening shoes to the tip of my trowel for being so wonderful to wear for all these years.*

*With a shared love of gardening,*
*Carol*

# CHAPTER 9

## SPEED WEEDING IN THE GARDEN

Weeding at top speeds approaching more than 20 weeds a minute, I once speed weeded my way through my large garden area called The Shrubbery.

I did not stop to choose a special weeding tool to dig up any weeds. I put on a good, thick pair of work gloves and pulled and tugged on weeds as fast as I could. If a weed didn't give up its grip of the earth with a solid tug, I cut it off at ground level. Fast, faster, *fastest* I went, until I had cleared the area entirely of weeds, at least on the surface.

I knew my satisfaction with seeing that area of the garden without weeds would be short-lived, and I accepted that. I just wanted the momentary satisfaction of seeing what this particular garden border would look like without mulberry tree seedlings coming up through the lilacs, without thistles crowding out the shrub roses, daring me with their thorns to pull them. I didn't want to wait.

I told myself as I speed weeded that I would return sooner rather than later to pull out the new weed sprouts that would surely crack through the surface in a week or so. Maybe I would even attempt to dig up their roots the next time. But I made no promises, even to myself, that I would actually do any of that. I know myself. I know that if my past behavior is an indication of what I'll do in the future—and it is—I really won't try to dig out those weed roots. But I am happy to say that I will try—time, weather, and my mind permitting.

I identified some of the weeds as I pulled them. There were plenty of thistles, some lamb's quarters, my ol' nemesis purslane, and too many mulberry saplings to count. There were also some dreadful nutsedges and foxtails tall enough to tickle my chin. And standing large and unafraid was a giant pokeweed. Pulling and cutting, none of the weeds were safe from my speed weeding.

Speed weeding isn't for everyone. It doesn't work for perfectionists who are bothered knowing those weed roots are still there. I have news for them. Even if they take the time to choose the perfect tools to dig up their weeds and take the extra time to do so, they will never get them all.

Speed weeding also doesn't work for timid or new gardeners. There is no time when speed weeding to look at each plant and ask "friend or foe" before pulling it. When you are speed weeding, if you pull up a good plant—and you are likely to do so at least once—you replant it, pat the soil around it, apologize to it, and move on.

I love an evening of speed weeding and being able to see progress right away. Too much of life deals with what we can't see, and it is difficult to know if we did good, made enough progress, or went fast enough. With speed weeding, you know right away that you are making progress; you can measure your speed, and you can see that the garden is better when you are finished.

I highly recommend it and its companion activities of speed planting and speed harvesting.

# CHAPTER 10

# PLANT MANNERS, OR A LACK THEREOF

I need to address the poor manners of some of the plants around my garden. I don't want to point trowels in any particular direction, but I believe doing so will help other gardeners.

Of course, the worst manners belong to the weeds. They usually arrive at this party known as my garden with nary an introduction. Then they stand around the buffet table partaking of the nutrients and sunshine while the invited guests, the plants I actually planted, languish nearby nearly starving for lack of the nutrients and sunshine those weeds are stealing from them. The weeds have worse manners than wedding crashers on their worst days.

It isn't just the weeds that have bad manners, as every gardener knows. I've got raspberries behaving as though they are briars, creeping—no, leaping—well beyond the bed I planted them in. And when they do that they invade the space I alloted to some nearby shrubs.

Well-behaved shrubs, I might add. Shrubs with good

manners, such as a pearl bush and a lilac. The only thing they do is drop their flower petals, which in most garden societies wouldn't be considered poor manners. It's cute and makes me smile, like you smile at a baby eating cake for the first time and getting some of it on the floor.

Other plants show their poor manners by shaking their seeds all over the garden. Asters do that. Then there are asters everywhere. Sure, violas do it too. But violas are sweet and little and I actually encourage their self-sowing. But not the asters. It's just rude when they show up clear on the other side of the garden, like the houseguest who wanders into that back bedroom, opening the door you thought you had locked so no one could see the mess.

And trees? Inviting an oak tree to grow in your garden is like inviting a dinner guest who drops their food one piece at a time throughout the entire dinner, and then gets up after dinner and leaves a trail of food crumbs all the way out of the house. The oak tree drops its leaves all fall, all winter, and well into spring until new young leaves finally push the last lingering leaves off. No sense in trying to clean up until the dinner is over and everyone has gone.

But I would never have a garden without these ill-mannered plants, well, except for the weeds. Weeds cannot be excused for their poor manners. But for all the other plants in the garden, I can forgive them for a shower of flower petals, a little self-sowing, a little spreading, a little lingering leaf drop.

They all give the garden a wonderful, lived-in

look, the kind of look that invites guests to linger long after dinner. It's a place where guests feel comfortable enough to take off their shoes and stay awhile, enjoying the flowers and the essence of a messy Mother Nature throughout the garden.

That's the kind of garden I like, the kind of garden I have, a garden filled with ill-mannered, imperfect, but well-loved plants, where guests and gardeners hopefully feel comfortable enough to stay awhile.

# CHAPTER 11

# IF PLANTS HAD BOOTS INSTEAD OF ROOTS

If plants had boots instead of roots, would they stay in your garden or would they put their boots on and move out? Why would they move out and look for a better place?

For starters, there is the weather forecast. After a spring weekend of record warm weather causes everyone to believe that winter is finally over, around my garden the weather forecast can quickly change to include words like snow, sleet, wind, and ice. Then all those foolish plants that popped up and bloomed early might be checking the schedule for a southbound bus if they had boots instead of roots.

And then there are the weeds. Who wants to live in a neighborhood where thistles flex their thorns at every leaf that grows within an inch of them? Who wants to put down roots in a spot where, if you aren't careful, a dandelion seed can germinate practically on top of you and then entwine its roots with your roots? I'm sure even the hardiest, toughest plant in the garden shudders at the thought.

Or how about location? Just as in real estate, location, location, location is important to many plants. If they had boots instead of roots, would plants run out of that low spot that seems to hold water for days on end after a rain? Would they move away from that tree that hogs all the moisture, sunlight, and nutrients, leaving them with nothing to grow on?

If plants had boots instead of roots and any sense of style, would they run away from that coral-colored flower that nothing else matches? Would they try to organize themselves a bit, like birds of a feather, in a way that makes them happy?

In some ways, plants *do* have boots in addition to roots. They can creep along, seed along, root along, and somehow move themselves around the garden, coming up in the oddest places. They can also just disappear, leaving the gardener to wonder if it was the weather, the weeds, the location, the other plants around them, or something else that drove them out. What caused them to exit the garden?

We may never know, but we ought to treat plants as if they have boots instead of roots. We should give them the best soil, the best location, and the best neighbors we can find for them. Then maybe they'll take off their boots, set down some roots, and stay awhile.

# CHAPTER 12

## IDEAS GROW IN THE WINTER GARDEN

Every winter I plant seeds for ideas to harvest and use in the garden.

Ideas are pretty easy to grow. They don't seem to mind the cold temperatures. In fact, sometimes they grow best on the coldest days when I'm inside reading gardening books. And if it snows and I can't go anywhere? That's when I usually see a lot of growth on the ideas I'm planning for my garden.

I fertilize my ideas with liberal doses of seed catalogs. Some seed catalogs are better fertilizer than others, but all provide some value. For a big boost, I'll supercharge the ideas growing in my garden by going to a gardening program and listening to others talk about gardening and plants. It never fails. I've come home from some of those programs to find gigantic ideas growing in the garden.

When the ideas in my garden start to reach full size, I encourage them to multiply and sow themselves about. After all, can you have too many good ideas in the garden? I don't think you can.

Late winter, as the winds die down and spring shows

signs of arriving, is when many of my ideas are almost ripe and ready to pick. Picking ideas for the garden sometimes involves making a few phones calls to line up help or convincing your significant other to help. Or you can harvest the ideas yourself if you have the time and energy.

Some gardeners prune their ideas back. I'm not sure why they do that. I think ideas grow best without pruning them or constraining them. Let them grow as they will, I say. After all, ideas are free and don't really cost anything until you actually harvest them.

When you do harvest your ideas, some may be bigger than you can manage, even with help. If that's the case, you can trim those ideas back a little and still have a good idea to plant in the garden later in the spring. Or if you have too many ideas, share them with other gardeners.

If you don't like some of the ideas you picked or don't feel like they are a good fit for your own garden, consider an idea swap. The ideas you don't think are right for your garden might be perfect for another person's garden. And their ideas might be just what you were seeking for your own garden.

There really is an unlimited supply of ideas for the garden. In fact, the unlimited supply can be overwhelming and confusing to many gardeners. If you feel overwhelmed or confused by the number of ideas in your garden, consider just setting some of your ideas aside for another time. But be aware that when and if you do set aside ideas for the garden, they can disappear on you. If that happens, you probably didn't need that idea anyway.

Whatever you do, don't avoid growing garden ideas in winter or any other season, because I think ideas add much to a garden and make each one unique.

# CHAPTER 13

## GOODBYE, STELLA

*Dear Stella,*

*May I get right to the point of this letter? It's time for you to go, Stella. Life is too short and the garden is too small to give you all the space you are taking.*

*Hemerocallis 'Stella de Oro', you've gone all commercial on me! I see you everywhere. You've grown common. You'll put down roots anyplace. So it's time. It's just time for us to part ways, for me to say goodbye to you.*

*But it's not all your fault, Stella. It's me too. Don't make me admit it! I'm not ashamed. Yes, I've been to a local daylily garden and well, it isn't that I don't like you anymore, it's that you've become so common and yellow compared to other daylilies. The others are so pretty and come in so many other shapes and colors. I've seen the others in colors ranging from pink to orange, even purple and maroon. And their shapes! You wouldn't believe their shapes. Some are ruffled, some have long narrow petals, and others are just so much bigger than you, Stella.*

*In comparison, you are just small and yellow. And you really are everywhere and not just everywhere in my garden. Every time I turn around, I see you. You're at the mall, at every gas station, and in front of nearly every commercial building in town.*

*With all your wanderings I guess we've just grown apart. And now I need your space for my new daylilies, the ones I'm going to have once you move out.*

*Stella, don't make this so hard on me! Stop blooming, darn it.*

*Oh, don't wilt. I'm sorry!*

*Okay, Stella, you can stay, but not in the prime spots in the garden. I'll tuck you in here and there, maybe give parts of you to some of the neighbors. After all, you do bloom and rebloom, and you bloom early. You were one of the first flowers in this garden. How could I get rid of you completely? Your flowers are kind of pretty, and I guess it isn't entirely your fault everyone likes you and you ended up so common.*

*Just promise you'll behave around the new daylilies, okay? And it would be good if you could teach some of them your re-blooming trick.*

*Love,*

*Carol*

# CHAPTER 14

## DEAREST SUMMER

*Dearest Summer,*

*I feel compelled to write to you this winter after your absence these last several months to tell you how much I miss you and how I long for your return.*

*I miss your music: the hum of the bees as they flew from flower to flower and the songs of the birds each morning, coaxing the sun to rise once again from the horizon. I so enjoyed, too, the sound of the water gurgling in the garden fountain. I would even like to hear the whirr of the lawn mower again.*

*I miss your warm breezes and the soft rain you brought with you, not just to break up the monotony of one sunny day after the next, but to water the plants in the garden.*

*Oh, the garden! Do you remember, Summer, when you presented me with the first green bean, the first ripe tomato, and the first ear of corn? I was so grateful. Did I tell you how grateful I was? Did I tell you how much I miss all that now, Summer?*

*I am not completely bereft in your absence, though. Winter has not mistreated me, so far. Winter has given me a chance to rest, to not feel the pressures you sometimes put* upon me to mow or water or just go outside to enjoy your sunshine and warmth.

Winter has also stuffed my mailbox full of seed catalogs.

But when I look through the seed catalogs, all I do is think of you, Summer. As I turn each page and see pictures of flowers and vegetables, I long for the days when we'll be together again.

Winter has changed me! For the better, I think. You'll see, Summer, how wonderful it is going to be when we are together again. I'm going to be a better person, a better gardener than I was when we were last together because, dearest Summer, Winter has given me a chance to think, to reflect, to plan, to vow to do better.

For starters, I'm going to be more diligent about weeding in the garden for you. I was so lax with it when we were last together and I admit you looked terrible at times as a result of my laziness. It was entirely my fault. But no longer. I will weed. I promise.

I also promise not to leave plants in their tiny nursery containers for days, weeks, even months at a time. When I buy you new plants, Summer, I promise to plant them right away or as soon as I possibly can. You can count on it, dearest Summer.

And I won't leave your produce out in the garden where it does no one any good. I will pick everything and share it with others, Summer, because it disrespects all you've done in the vegetable garden when I don't.

Finally, I promise that when you return I won't complain about your hot days. I know you can't help them. And I will definitely cherish any rain you bring. Please *count on that, Summer, just as I count the days until your return.*

*In the meantime while I wait and bide my time with Winter, I'll continue to look through the seed catalogs, which remind me so much of you, Summer, and make plans for your return.*

*With more fondness than you can imagine,*
*Carol*

# CHAPTER 15

# DEAR DROUGHT

*Dear Drought,*

*Please consider this letter your notice of eviction from my garden. You are hereby and forthwith ordered to vacate the premises immediately upon receipt of this letter and leave behind any substance that is composed of two hydrogen molecules and one oxygen molecule, such as and including moisture, rainfall, dew, and any other types of precipitation that may fall on the garden at any time now and in the future.*

*You are also commanded to take with you all above-normal temperatures.*

*This notice of eviction is rightly and fairly given due to your withholding of all rain and other forms of precipitation due in June and July, when in fact you owed 4.13 inches for June and 4.42 inches for July for a total deficit of 8.53 inches for just those two months alone.*

*In addition, you made a complete mess of the garden, evidence of which I can send at your request.*

*Though I am aware that you provided 2 inches of rain as recently as early August, this does not make up for the heartache and distress you have caused for most* of the summer nor is it evidence of any intent to reform your behavior in future months. There is still a deficit of at least 6.53 inches, plus the additional amount you owe for August.

I thereby request that you leave my garden in an orderly fashion so as not to cause any further disturbance in the garden or in the heart of the gardener by any means including wind, heat, and so forth.

Should you not vacate my garden as requested and leave behind adequate rainfall, I will not be responsible for my actions henceforth, actions such as wailing and gnashing of teeth.

Firmly stated,
Carol

# CHAPTER 16

## COMPOST BY THE SEA

I watched as the old man picked up seaweed along the beach. He moved gingerly while reaching for the seaweed with long tongs, the kind generally used to pick up trash. As he put the seaweed in one of his two five-gallon buckets, I looked up and down the shoreline, covered with seaweed.

Surely he wasn't trying to clear the beach of all the seaweed? I was curious. I politely asked him what he was going to do with the seaweed.

"It's for my compost pile."

Of course. Compost. I immediately contemplated picking up some seaweed for my own compost pile, 800 miles away.

Then I realized I had nothing to put the seaweed in, and it might start to smell on the drive home. When I stopped at a rest stop along the highway, how would I explain the rotting smell coming from my car?

We can all agree compost piles shouldn't really smell bad if created properly. We can also agree that a plastic trash bag filled with seaweed thrown inside the trunk of a car and carted hundreds of miles away is not the proper way to create compost.

The proper way to make compost is with locally sourced plant debris from one's own garden and maybe the neighboring gardens, including some brown plant debris and some green plant debris, but no disease- or insect-infested plant debris. And no seed-laden weeds. Also, no meat products of any kind or pet poo in a compost pile. That's just asking for trouble.

We turn the piles if we have the opportunity and the inclination to do so, or leave them as is and wait. Eventually, all kinds of little critters ranging from microscopic organisms to big fat earthworms will feast on that organic matter, turning it into compost—beautiful, rich, earthy-smelling compost. I call it black gold.

My three compost bins are pretty full year-round. I seem to be too busy most of the time to harvest the black gold compost that is waiting for me under this year's contributions until the end of the gardening season. By then the compost is usually reaching a platinum level.

I always look forward to digging into those compost bins when the days get a little cooler, harvesting the compost and spreading it about the garden, while dreaming of how next year's vegetable crops will thrive in its richness. Then I promptly fill the bins back up with the gleanings of the garden after a good, hard frost. I've learned I don't need to bring home seaweed from my vacation for the compost bins. I have everything I need right here.

CHAPTER 17

## THERE'S MAGIC IN A CLOVER LAWN

There's magic in a clover lawn, and every person who remembers being a child recognizes that magic.

In a clover lawn you can carefully pick the flowers and tie them together to make bracelets and necklaces and long flower chains. You can create a tiara fit for a queen and then you are transformed into the Queen of the Garden. All the garden fairies will gather 'round to grant you your fondest wishes and dreams. You can sit for hours staring at the three-leaf clovers until magically, a four-leaf clover appears before your eyes.

With that four-leaf clover you will have the most marvelous day, filled with all kinds of good luck. And later you can carefully place the four-leaf clover between the pages of a book, and put the book on a shelf. Then on a cold winter's day, you can open that book to the page with the clover leaf to bring you even more joy and good luck.

In a clover lawn you can watch for hours as bees show up, seemingly out of nowhere, to visit each and every bloom, eager to get to the sweet nectar contained within.

Yes, there's magic in a clover lawn. The clover will

even fix nitrogen in the soil and share its nutrients with the grass to make it greener.

So if we believe there's magic in a clover lawn—and there is no reason not to—why don't people want clover in their lawns today?

Once upon a time, people did not realize what magic there was in a clover lawn. They never thought about it. They just assumed all lawns had clover growing in them. Then a villain came by and commented with just a bit of a sneer about how nice it might look if the lawns were all grass with no clover at all.

And the people looked at their lawns and thought perhaps the villain, whom they didn't realize was a villain at the time, was right. Their lawns might look nice if they were all green with no clover.

Then the villain explained how they could put something on their lawns to make the clover go away, and the clover would stay away as long as they put it on every single year. I'm sure this villain wasn't wearing all black and smiling with an evil, sinister grin when he sold them that something, a poison, to get rid of the clover, but it's fun to imagine that's what he looked like.

As the years went by, one person after the next bought the poison from the villain and put it on their lawns. The villain got richer and richer and the people became poorer and poorer. The poor people. They didn't even realize how poor they had become when they had no more clover in their lawns.

When the poison killed off all the clover, everyone thought they would be so happy with their lawns all green and grassy. No one realized that when the clover disappeared so did the magic: the tiaras and four-leaf clovers, the long flower chains, even clover bracelets and necklaces. They were all gone. The bees left too. And nothing in the lawn fixed the nitrogen the way the clover did.

Yes, the lawns were green, but they contained no magic.

In defense of the people, they did not know the magic was actually in the clover. They believed the villain.

But gradually, the people started to figure it out. They figured out the magic was gone and that the magic came from the clover. So they stopped buying the villain's poisons.

Fortunately, once they stopped using the villain's poisons, the clover began to return. And when the clover came back, it brought with it the magic: the tiaras and four-leaf clovers, the long flower chains, the bracelets and necklaces. And the bees came back too. And, yes, other flowers joined the clover in the lawn, like dandelions and violets and even plantain.

But the people didn't mind the extra flowers. The people rejoiced when the magic returned and vowed never to let the villain trick them like that again.

CHAPTER 18

# BEAUTY AND THE VEGETABLE FEAST

Once upon a garden, there was a gardener named Flora who had a beautiful garden full of flowers. Flora loved her garden and spent many hours tending it. And when it wasn't too hot, Flora even liked to sit in her garden and enjoy all the flowers.

One beautiful summer day, Flora was sitting in her garden smiling and enjoying all the flowers. She looked around and slowly her smile turned into a frown. "Something is missing in my garden, and I can't quite put my finger on what it is," she said to no one in particular.

Just then a huge bee flew by and caught Flora's attention. Such a bee she had never seen. It paused in front of her, and when it had her attention, it flew off a couple of feet and then came back. The bee did this several times before Flora realized, "I think this bee wants me to follow him."

So she got up and followed the bee to the edge of the garden where there was a giant hedge. The bee flew into the hedge, but Flora stopped. She had never been on the other side of the hedge, and so she had no idea what was over there. Soon the bee came out again, and this time he flew around Flora and chased her right into the hedge.

With a little scream, Flora fell through the hedge and landed on the other side. Shaken, she got up and looked around. She was pretty sure she was in a garden, but it wasn't like any flower garden she'd ever seen.

"Where am I?" she asked.

"You're in a vegetable garden," answered the bee.

Flora looked around to see who was talking before she realized it was the bee.

"Bees don't talk!" she exclaimed.

"Well, we do in vegetable gardens," said the bee.

"Is that where I am?" Flora asked. And looking around, she said with awe, "I didn't know vegetable gardens could look like this."

"They can indeed look like this," said the bee. "Let me show you around."

And the bee began to lead her around the vegetable garden. They stopped first at a row of radishes.

"Taste this," said the bee, pulling a radish out of the ground, wiping it off, and handing it to her.

Flora looked at it suspiciously but did as the bee asked. "Oh," she said. "That's so crisp and has a nice kick to it. I've never tasted a radish so good."

The bee didn't respond but led her to the cucumber patch. He picked a cucumber that was much smaller than those big, club-sized cucumbers Flora bought at the grocery store. Flora dutifully bit into the cucumber and couldn't help but smile. "Wow," she said. "Is that what real cucumbers taste like? They don't grow with that wax on them?"

The bee nodded and moved on to the sweet corn patch. He pulled off an ear of corn, shucked it, and handed it to Flora. "Don't we need to cook it first?" asked Flora.

The bee answered, "No, try it."

So Flora bit into the ear of sweet corn and exclaimed to the bee, "How sweet!"

The bee nodded knowingly.

Next, they stopped and picked some green beans. Flora had never known how crunchy fresh raw green beans could be.

In the nearby pea patch, Flora stopped and said she didn't like peas, and there was no way she was eating them. But the bee insisted, and so she tasted some. "Those are the sweetest green jewels I've ever eaten!" she exclaimed.

Flora then saw some exotic-looking flowers on the edge of one of the garden beds. "What are those?" Flora asked.

"Okra flowers," answered the bee.

"Oh, I don't like okra," said Flora.

"You would if you grew it yourself and picked it when it was little," said the bee.

Next, they paused at some pretty orange flowers. "What are these?" asked Flora. "I've never seen flowers like these."

"Those are edible flowers, nasturtiums, actually," said the bee.

Edible? Flora was skeptical but tried one and said they tasted like pepper.

"Oh, look over there," Flora said. "Now, those are flowers."

Indeed, there were zinnias growing by the edge of the garden.

"Those are for us bees," said the bee. "They make sure we find the garden so we can pollinate the squash and other vegetables. And if you don't mind, I'm pretty tired and hungry from luring you into this garden and showing you around. Sit down over there while I rest on this flower and snack on its nectar."

So Flora sat down and began to think about growing vegetables while the bee gobbled up the nectar from the zinnia. She turned to the bee and said, "Can I ask you a few questions?"

"Of course," buzzed the bee, now covered in pollen.

"Well, I thought vegetable gardens were a lot of work," said Flora.

"Don't you work hard in your flower garden, Flora?" responded the bee.

"And I thought vegetable gardens weren't pretty, either."

"Oh, Flora, who told you that? Vegetable gardens can be so pretty."

"But what if I don't have room for vegetables?" asked Flora.

"Well, you can grow them in containers on your patio," answered the bee.

"Good idea," said Flora, "but where are the tomatoes?

I thought all vegetable gardens had tomatoes in them."

"Over here," said the bee, as he led her to the center of the vegetable garden.

"Oh, how pretty they are!" exclaimed Flora as she reached down to pick one.

"Be careful," warned the bee. "If you eat that tomato, it will change your life. You will never rest or be happy in your garden again until you grow tomatoes and vegetables."

"Oh, I don't know about that," said Flora.

And slowly she lifted the tomato up to her mouth. The bee covered his eyes and looked away as Flora closed her eyes and slowly bit into the tomato. She could taste the warmth of the sun and feel the juice of the tomato slowly drip down her chin. She smiled as she realized she had never tasted anything like it in her entire life.

Just then she opened her eyes and realized she was back in her flower garden, sitting on her bench. "Oh my," said Flora, "I must grow vegetables. Such a thought! Where did that come from and why am I holding this half-eaten tomato?"

She hardly noticed the little bee sitting next to her, smiling, as she looked around her garden to see where she could grow vegetables. In a field, in raised beds, in containers, or even among the flowers, she did not care. She knew she had to grow vegetables.

And she gardened happily ever after.

CHAPTER 19

# A GARDENER'S GUIDE TO TEMPORARY BOTANICAL NAMES

A friend of mine, who knows not a whit about gardening, likes to test my knowledge of plants by pointing at a tree or shrub or flower and asking, "What's that?" Then I fire back with the botanical and common names of the plant and she responds that I could be making up the name and she would never know.

She's right. I could be making up the name and she and many others would be none the wiser. In fact, I actually find it useful to know a few temporary botanical names to use in those situations where I don't know the actual botanical name of the plant.

Using temporary names sounds smarter than "uh, uh, uh", if you feel the need to sound smart, and serves as a placeholder of sorts until you have a chance either to remember the real botanical name or look it up. No harm done, unless of course your friend actually remembers the temporary name and uses it to sound smart in front of others.

Regardless, I have a fallback list of temporary names.

*Forgetia*, pronounced "for-get-ee-ya." I use this genus name along with an appropriate descriptive species name when I have honestly forgotten the botanical name. Later I will spend some time searching online or looking in reference books to jog my memory.

For example, *Forgetia rosea* might be a plant with a pink flower. Or *Forgetia giantosa* might be the biggest plant in your garden, the one you can't believe you can't remember the botanical name for.

*Lookupsia*, pronounced "look-up-sia." I find this to be a useful temporary genus name when I know I've recorded the name of the plant in my garden journal, and I just need a minute to go in and look it up. Again, you can combine it with any descriptive species name so it sounds more complete.

For example, *Lookupsia orchida* is a good temporary name for the hardy orchid I planted years ago, the one I can never remember the name of when it first pops up in spring until I look it up in my garden journal. Then I can remember it for the rest of the season until the long winter wipes it from my memory again.

*Neverknewia*, pronounced "nev-er-new-ia." I think this name is most useful when you are visiting a garden and you really have no idea what a plant's name is. Perhaps it is a garden in a different climate from your own, where many of the plants may be new to you. You are one lucky gardener to be visiting gardens in other climates.

Eventually, some other person will come along and ask you what is. You can answer "*Neverknewia plantsia*" in a soft little voice, and then they may politely correct you saying, "Really, it looks more like a rose to me." At that moment you can drop the temporary botanical name and loudly call it by its real botanical name, *Rosa* (or whatever it turns out to be).

*Weedisia*, pronounced "wee-de-sia." I use this genus name when someone asks me the name of a plant I am pretty sure is a weed I should have pulled. Then, when the other person isn't looking or has left the garden, if it is my garden, I pull that darn weed. And absolutely, even if they beg, I do not dig and divide it and give it to them as a passalong plant.

For example, *Weedisia prolifica* would probably work for most weeds because most weeds are usually prolific.

Now if you think all these temporary botanical names are just foolishness and want to know how to avoid being in situations where you feel you need to use one of them, I have one suggestion—visit gardens by yourself. But what's the fun of that? There is no shame in not knowing the names of every plant you see, even if you are the world's best gardener or a trained horticulturist. No one can know every plant in the plant kingdom by its botanical name.

So for those times when you don't know the name of a plant, give it a temporary name, at least until you have a chance to figure out what it really is.

CHAPTER 20

# COMMON MALADIES

When I am out in my garden deep in thought, my internal therapist, whom I've named Dr. Hortfreud, helps me work through problems, come up with good ideas, and keeps me on the straight and narrow path in the garden. At least she tries to. I attribute to her, my inner garden therapist, this list of maladies that many gardeners suffer from.

**Plant Lust** is one of the most common maladies. Gardeners are likely to come down with a bad case of Plant Lust anytime they enter the garden of another gardener and see a lovely plant they do not have. Symptoms include lingering in front of the plant for long periods of time, asking a barrage of questions about the plant, most notably, "Where can I get that?" and immediately feeling deprived because they don't have that plant in their own gardens. They may not have known five minutes before that such a plant even existed, but now that they've seen it, they vow they cannot go on without it.

In extreme cases of Plant Lust, some gardeners may attempt to remove seed pods or pinch off a tiny cutting in hopes of rooting it for their own garden. However, every gardener knows or soon learns that stolen seeds, cuttings, or even plants will not grow in the thief's garden.

**Cart Eyes** is another form of Plant Lust that occurs in gardeners when they are shopping at a garden center or greenhouse and notice a plant on another gardener's cart and immediately desire to have that particular plant or one just like it. The onset of Cart Eyes can be quite sudden and may cause a gardener to purchase a plant they previously had not noticed and have no idea where in their garden they will plant it once they take it home.

In rare cases, Cart Eyes can induce a gardener to attempt to distract a shopper who has the plant they desire so they can swipe that plant from the shopper's cart or quickly switch it for another one.

While on the subject of plant shopping, everyone should be aware of **Forgotten About**, which happens when gardeners are so overcome by plant shopping that they forget about the size of their car and buy more plants than they can reasonably fit into it. The remedy, of course, is to unreasonably pack the car. Or they forget that they came with other people who will need to ride home in the car that is now full of plants. This is usually cured by placing plants on everyone's laps once they are seated.

Forgotten About also occurs when gardeners return to their gardens with all of their plant purchases and realize they have also forgotten about the size of their garden, the plants they had previously purchased and not yet planted, and all the plants they already have in their garden. They now wonder where they will plant everything they just purchased. In extreme cases, some gardeners may take over planting in adjoining properties.

Any gardener who leaves their garden and travels to a warmer climate or sometimes a much colder climate runs the risk of coming down with a case of **Zone Envy**, also known as **Zone Denial**. Seeing a plant that simply will not survive in one's own climate zone is almost torture for some gardeners. Those gardeners often become **Zone Pushers**, coming up with all kinds of protections and techniques that look like plain ol' hard work to get those plants to grow, or in some cases, merely survive in their gardens. There is no cure for Zone Envy as long as gardeners remain in their own zones, though finding the warmest microclimate in a garden helps a little.

**Sunny** is a recently named malady that affects gardeners when the weather conditions are perfect for gardening, as in 63 degrees Fahrenheit and sunny. It is worse when the preceding days were 45 degrees Fahrenheit and rainy, and the 63-degree-and-sunny day occurs on a weekend. Once a gardener comes down with Sunny, it is best for everyone if they are allowed to cancel all other plans and spend the day in the garden.

Attempting to force the gardener to do other activities, especially indoors, when they've come down with a case of Sunny can result in mental harm to the gardener. Symptoms may include grumpiness, frowny face, and in some cases withering stares toward the person or thing that caused them to miss out on a day in the garden. Sunny most often occurs in early spring and late fall. It is rare in the heat of summer.

Though none of these gardener's maladies are life threatening, my inner therapist, Dr. Hortfreud, notes it is important to recognize their existence and treat them promptly for the health and well being of the gardener and all those around them.

# CHAPTER 21

# GADS

Garden Attention Distraction Syndrome (GADS) is a common affliction amongst gardeners. If you follow a gardener around for even an hour, you'll notice the symptoms. If you are a gardener, you may notice the symptoms in yourself.

Perhaps you've just cleaned up your houseplants, and like a good gardener, you tossed all the trimmings and the potting soil from that long-dead plant you finally decided will not revive itself into a plastic tub to haul out to your growing compost pile.

As soon as you step outside, you see a giant weed and wonder why you never pulled it. You decide that now is the time to pull that weed. "GADS," you think to yourself, "I need to pull that weed." So you proceed to pull that weed and then see something else to be done, like maybe some zinnias that call out to be cut and brought inside. "GADS, those are so pretty." So you leave the tub next to the bed with the pulled weed and go get your pruners.

Going and getting your pruners can involve the gardener's version of Hide and Seek, which is often played with gardening tools, especially small hand tools like pruners and trowels which never seem to be where you last put them or even where you swore you were going to put them whenever you were finished with them. Eventually, though, you find your pruners, and assuming the hunt did not distract you with some other gardening task, you make your way back to the zinnias and cut a few to take inside. "GADS, that took longer than expected."

Once inside, you may end up in another game called Find the Perfect Vase. While playing Find the Perfect Vase, you suddenly notice some drooping houseplants, so you decide you had better water them lest they suffer the fate of the dead houseplant that got you started on your day of gardening. "GADS, I had better water those houseplants."

Once you find your watering can, you fill it with water, water the houseplants, and, as often happens, spill some of the water onto the floor. That leads you to decide to go ahead and clean up the entire floor because, GADS, it has been awhile since you mopped it, what with all your time spent in the garden. By the time you finish mopping, it is nighttime and there isn't enough daylight to go back out to the garden to do what you had started to do in the first place.

The next morning you go outside to the garden and see that the tub of trimmings and potting soil that you were going to take out to the compost bin yesterday is still sitting right next to where you pulled that big weed. You think, "GADS, I need to dump that in the compost bin."

Congratulations, you've come full circle through an attack of Gardeners Attention Distraction Syndrome.

Is it any wonder that anything ever gets finished in a garden?

Are there cures for this malady? There are no cures that I know of, so I just enjoy the process. I don't mind spending a morning wandering from task to task, doing whatever I think needs to be done in the garden. It's nice in many ways not to feel like the day must be spent focused on a Big Gardening Project.

Of course, there are times when a Big Gardening Project is called for. Then it's good to put on your virtual blinders, shut off all access to social media, round up your tools, and dig in. You might still end up doing something else and losing focus but, GADS, at least you know you are in the company of other good gardeners who suffer with you.

# CHAPTER 22

# MOTIVATION

We all start out the gardening season full of ideas and energy with Motivation at our side. Then one day we find ourselves standing in the middle of the garden on a hot summer day and notice Motivation is gone. Did you ever wonder where the Motivation to garden goes in the summertime?

On the first warm day of early spring, we grab our little friend, Motivation, roll up our sleeves, and dig into the garden once again. We hold hands with Motivation and walk around the garden, together marveling how the soil is so soft and crumbly and smells just like we remembered it smelling. We are excited it is finally spring. We are in love with our gardens, and Motivation is right there with us.

We take Motivation with us to the garden centers where it encourages us to buy plants by the flats and load up our trunks and trucks with mulch and topsoil. We can hardly wait to take it all home and transform our gardens once again with Motivation's help. We are just so productive with Motivation by our side. We can hardly bear to see the sun set, forcing us back inside with Motivation to wait impatiently for another dawn and another day of gardening.

Then one day, it happens. Motivation disappears. It's hot. There are mosquitoes. Motivation doesn't like heat and mosquitoes. Motivation gets discouraged, too, because not everything turned out as we thought it would. Motivation likes pretty flowers, but runs and hides at the sight of weeds.

We think occasionally we ought to go look for Motivation in the summertime and see if we can get it to help us do a little weeding, but then we go for a few weeks without rain. We know that even if we find it, Motivation will whine and try to convince us to wait until it rains before we weed and may even suggest if we wait, the bigger weeds will be easier to see and pull out.

Motivation can be tricky that way.

Then we sort of get used to not having Motivation around in the dog days of summer.

We occasionally get a glimpse of our ol' spring friend Motivation when the first green beans are ready to be picked. And Motivation is always there eager to taste the first ripe tomatoes, the first ears of sweet corn, the first of any crop.

Then Motivation realizes again that it's hot and there are mosquitoes and goes into hiding once more. Where does our friend Motivation hide? Motivation likes to hide in the cucumber patch and looks a lot like overripe cucumbers. It disguises itself as "something green" in the back of the flower border, which, on closer inspection, is nothing more than our old nemesis, Thistle.

Good ol' Motivation. It likes to leave us with just enough of itself to mow the lawn but not enough to trim the lawn because Motivation is like that.

Fortunately, at least in my garden, Motivation usually shows up again around Labor Day. It's ready to weed those paths, trim the lawn, and clear out the overgrown cucumbers. Truthfully, I think Motivation is just a little bit embarrassed by how it let the weeds grow and didn't provide a proper support for the wisteria—again. Motivation is ready to make amends, start all over again, and renew our relationship. And no matter what happened all summer, no matter where Motivation hid when it was hot and buggy, I'm ready to forgive and forget too. I'm happy when Motivation comes back in early fall. It's always welcome in my garden.

CHAPTER 23

## SHOPPING IN A GARDEN CENTER

I ran across a metaphor involving elephants that explained how we think emotionally and rationally at the same time. It immediately explained to me my own behavior when I am shopping at a garden center.

According to this metaphor, our emotional thinking when our instincts kick in is like an elephant. Our rational thinking, which applies reason and thinks about the long-term, is like a little rider on top of that elephant trying to control it.

Now picture when you go to a garden center and see a plant you love from a distance. The elephant in you awakens, rears up on its hind legs, trumpets loudly, and goes thundering toward that plant. Pity the casual shopper standing in your elephant's way, your emotional self, as you run instinctively in the direction of the plant, looking neither left nor right, until you finally grasp that plant in your trunk and trumpet out, "Mine, all mine."

Then picture the rider on the elephant who has been clinging on for dear life until the elephant finally has the plant in their grasp. Now the rider gets their turn and regains control of the elephant. The rider starts to ask questions. Where are you going to plant that? Is it worth spending all the grocery money to have that plant? Do you really need it to be complete as a gardener?

Oh, that elephant rider can be such a downer. So practical. So logical. Occasionally, the rider lets the elephant buy the plant. Other times the rider eventually convinces the elephant to put the plant down, apologize to all the people they've stampeded past, and pick out a more realistic alternative.

But sometimes the elephant doesn't listen to the rider and won't let go of the plant. The elephant loves the plant and is taking it home to their garden regardless of what the rider does or says.

I have certainly enjoyed many rides through a garden center on my elephant. Sometimes the rider in me makes my elephant put down the plant. Fortunately, sometimes the rider stays quiet and lets the elephant in me buy my folly—I mean plant—and I'm grateful for that. It adds a bit of character, some pizazz, to our gardens if we sometimes allow our emotions to decide which plants to purchase.

After all, practical and logical choices do not always a surprising, fun garden make, though at times the rider has had to fix what the elephant did. I swear it was the elephant who bought 1,100 crocus corms to plant one fall, ignoring the rider trying to control it, calm it down, and convince it to settle for a more practical number. All the elephant could think of was how the crocuses would look blooming in the lawn in spring. I'm glad, though, that the elephant, the emotional one, got her way. The rider, the rational one, cleaned up the mess and figured out a way to plant all 1,100 crocuses in an afternoon. Both my elephant and my rider now look forward every spring to the time when the crocuses bloom in the lawn.

Watch out for your elephant and other elephants the next time you go to a garden center or tour a garden. You know who they are and how to spot them. And for goodness sake, stay out of the way if two elephants stampede toward the same plant. Or at least hope there are experienced riders on board who can come to a nice compromise on who actually gets that plant. Then take that plant home and thank your elephant and the rider for shopping with you at the garden center.

# CHAPTER 24

## BUYING SHRUBS

There are five types of shrub buyers.

*The Researcher*: Researchers know exactly what shrubs they want to buy, right down to the cultivar name. They've done their homework. They've done online searches for the shrubs they are interested in and cross-referenced that information with books and then double-checked their choices through online forums to make sure they've picked the perfect shrub. Then they spend more hours trying to find that exact shrub for sale.

*The Grabber*: Grabbers are the opposite of Researchers. They have no idea what they want other than "shrubs." They go to the garden centers or big box stores and pick shrubs with pretty blooms and leaves and comment, "It's green, good enough." And off they go with their shrubs, which, of course, they generally call "bushes" because they really don't know any better.

*The Rescuers*: Rescuers can usually be found hanging around the back of the garden center where broken, battered, and bruised plants are marked down to clear out. Rescuers are on a mission. They see those poor mistreated shrubs with half the soil knocked out of their containers, branches broken through mishandling, wilting with no water in the hot afternoon sun, and buy those. They are convinced that with a little pruning, a good drink of water, and some soothing garden talk those rescued shrubs will be just as nice and healthy as the other ones. Oh, and the money they saved!

*The Experimenters*: Experimenters are looking for "something different." They want to be on the cutting edge when it comes to shrubs. Who cares if no one has heard of the shrubs they are buying, or there is no information about those shrubs? So much the better. They are willing to take a chance to be the first to have those shrubs. They are willing to push the shrubs a zone or two beyond their published hardiness zone. Common shrubs? Please. Experimenters would rather buy annuals than have common shrubs in their gardens.

*The Gardeners*: Gardeners can be a bit unpredictable and be all types of shrub buyers—Researchers, Grabbers, Rescuers, Experimenters—all in the same trip to the garden center.

Gardeners often go in as Researchers, looking for a specific shrub and the next thing they know, they are Grabbers, putting a couple of shrubs on the cart because they are green and oh, yeah, there was that one bare spot that would be good to fill in with a few basic shrubs.

Then they pass the clearance shrubs, and even though they had promised themselves before heading to the garden center that they were going to stay away from the marked-down plants, there they are, Rescuers, saving just a few of them.

Finally, they wheel their carts toward the check-out area, loaded down with their one specific shrub, a few shrubs just because they are green, and another few shrubs that called out to be rescued when suddenly they stop and look down at the tag of a new shrub they've never seen before and purr in their special, low Experimenter voice, "Well, aren't you different? How would you like to come home with me?"

And then they load that shrub onto their cart, pay for their purchases, and head back to their gardens.

Researchers, Grabbers, Rescuers, Experimenters, Gardeners: They're all out there buying shrubs.

# CHAPTER 25

## RARE IN CULTIVATION

If you want to entice a gardener to buy a plant practically sight unseen, just mention it is "rare in cultivation." Those three words will cause any gardener's heart to skip a beat. Put "rare in cultivation" in writing and a gardener will practically start shaking as they keep reading to figure out what this plant is, other than rare in cultivation.

Before they know what this plant is, they are deciding where to plant it though they don't know yet if it is a tree, a shrub, a vegetable, or a flower. None of that matters because it is rare in cultivation so they must have it. They will begin scouring the internet looking for a source for it. They will lie awake at night scheming about how to get one of these plants for their own garden.

What will this plant cost? The gardener is hoping it won't be too costly. Perhaps another gardener already has one and is willing to share a cutting or seed for it. Maybe they can work out a trade for a plant they have that the other gardener wants. They go down a mental list of every gardener they know wondering who they can barter with. They are already planning who they can show their new plant to, casually mentioning, of course, that it is rare in cultivation, even before they have it.

Maybe this rare-in-cultivation plant they now must have won't cost so much that others in the family notice if they dip into rainy day funds to purchase it. After all, don't gardeners have rainy day funds just for this type of emergency purchase? Surely others will understand how their garden will now always be lacking if they do not have this plant that is rare in cultivation that they just heard about. Their purchase is justified!

And they are doing a good deed by purchasing this rare-in-cultivation plant. Their one purchase might entice those who grow it to increase the supply of this plant for all gardeners. They think how wonderful that would be and what a great contribution they are making to the gardening world by buying this plant so rare in cultivation.

The quandary for gardeners, though, is once there are more of these plants so rare in cultivation, they might lose their appeal. But most gardeners aren't thinking that far ahead. They are thinking that right now, it is rare in cultivation, and therefore they need it for their gardens.

Just those three magic words—rare in cultivation—is all it takes to make a gardener clamor for whatever the plant is. You can show a gardener a picture of a common weed like crabgrass and describe it as rare in cultivation, and they will want it. The crabgrass will suddenly yet erroneously be thought of as a plant that few other gardeners have, and therefore it is special to have such a plant.

After all, it is rare in cultivation.

# CHAPTER 26

# HOW WIDE TO MAKE YOUR
# GARDEN PATHS

*Dear Fellow Gardener,*

*How wide should the paths be in a vegetable garden?
Gardeners everywhere are asking this question. If your
garden paths are too narrow, they are useless to all but
rabbits and raccoons. If your garden paths are too wide,
you've wasted valuable planting space.*

*Some people say the paths should be wide enough for
two people to walk side by side. That may be true if the
path is designed for ambling through the garden arm in
arm with someone else, but who goes ambling arm in arm
with someone else through a vegetable garden?*

*Some people like narrow paths in a vegetable garden,
barely wide enough for you to shuffle sideways through the
garden, so you have more planting space. This only makes
sense if you like to shuffle sideways through the garden. In
my opinion, the sideways shuffle is an awkward way to get
around in the garden. And if it is awkward to do, then you
probably won't get around your garden regularly. You'll
probably abandon your garden, the weeds will take over,
everyone will think it is ugly, and no one will encourage*

*you to plant another vegetable garden, ever. "You'll just let it be taken over by weeds like the last time," they'll say, and you may never try to grow vegetables again.*

*I shudder at the thought of narrow paths leading to the demise of your garden, the dashing of your hopes, and no homegrown vegetables to eat all summer.*

*Others suggest the path needs to be wide enough for you to kneel in front of one bed without crunching the bed behind you with your backside.*

*Balderdash to all those answers! I've determined the perfect width for the paths in my vegetable garden and it is 19 inches.*

*How did I choose 19 inches, you ask?*

*That's the width of the stand, the legs, the whatever you call them, on my wheelbarrow, plus a half-inch on either side to set them down.*

*And now that I've set the width of the garden paths to work for my wheelbarrow, I'll be keeping that wheelbarrow for life.*

*With a shared love of gardening,*
*Carol*

CHAPTER 27

resources

# THE GARDENING EQUATION

Many gardeners take a certain analytical approach to gardening. They measure before they plant and never guess how much mulch they need before they order up even that first cubic yard. They figure out the area they are working with and how thick they want the mulch, and then they perform various calculations to determine the exact amount of mulch they need.

For those more analytical gardeners, and really all gardeners, I've developed a formula that I call the Gardening Equation to predict your overall satisfaction with your gardening experience.

The formula is $((S+P+C) \times D)+To+Ti+W+CU = GE$

Here is how to work this equation:

*Rate your Soil (S).* If you constantly have to remove rocks and other debris from your soil, wonder if maybe your garden was once a landfill, or think that a pickaxe is a good tool to use for digging, rate your soil around a 1. If your soil looks like crumbly, dark brown soil full of good compost and lovely earthworms and you want to weep with joy each time you dig through it with your bare hands, rate your soil a 10. If your soil is somewhere between those two types, decide which it most resembles and rate accordingly.

*Rate your Plants (P).* If you love all the plants in your garden and they are the exact plants you want to grow, rate your plants a 10. Conversely if you do not care for the plants in your garden, perhaps they came with the garden when you bought it and you want to rip them all out and start all over again, rate your plants a 1. If your feelings for your plants fall somewhere in between, perhaps you long for just a few plants that you've read about and haven't found to buy, rate accordingly.

*Rate your Climate (C).* If you love your climate and wonder why anyone would ever want to garden some place colder or warmer, wetter or drier, rate your climate a 10. If you are constantly looking at maps and checking real estate guides to figure out how to move to another climate, rate your climate a 1. If your feelings about your climate are not one extreme or another, rate accordingly.

*Rate your Design (D).* Design is either a 1 or a 2, or rarely a 0. If you have a pretty good design for your garden, rate your design a 2. If you don't have a design and feel like your plants are all misplaced, rate your design a 1. Only give yourself a 0 if you think a garden design is a waste of time. This is where you can also factor in the size of your garden. If it is a good design but too small or too large, drop the rating to a 1.

*Rate your Tools (To).* If you always have the tools you need for any gardening activity and you know how to use them to such a degree that when you garden you barely notice you are using tools, rate your tools a 10. If you are looking in your kids' sandbox for their plastic sand shovel because you can't find your trowel or you lack other decent tools, rate your tools a 1. Most of us fall in between, so rate your tools accordingly.

*Rate your Gardening Time (Ti).* If you feel like your garden is so needy that you will never be able to give it enough time, rate your time a 1. On the other extreme, if you feel like your garden requires just the amount of time you have to give it, rate your time a 10. If your feelings about the time you spend in your garden are somewhere between those two ends of the time spectrum, rate accordingly.

*Rate your Weeds (W).* This rating is a little tricky. If you have so many weeds you are thinking of pruning and deadheading them just to feel better about having them, rate your weeds a 1. If you rarely have weeds in your garden or you are able to remove weeds when they are teeny tiny before anyone else sees them, give yourself a 10 for weeds. If you fall in between these two scenarios, rate yourself accordingly.

*Rate your Chemical Usage (CU).* If you do not use chemicals on your garden, give yourself a 10 on this one. If you use so many chemicals that there are no beneficial insects buzzing around the flowers, the squirrels cross the street rather than walk through your garden, and the birds are flying by wearing gas masks, give yourself a 0 on this one. If your chemical usage falls in between, rate accordingly.

Now, add P, S, and C together and multiply that sum by D. Take that number and add in Ti, To, W, and CU. The result, GE, Gardening Enjoyment or Experience, will be a number less than 100 but greater than 1.

A 100 means you lied on your ratings. Go back and check that weed one for sure.

If you scored:

80 – 99: Wow. You've got this gardening thing all figured out. Good for you, but I think I might see a few weeds if I visited your garden, and I want a soil sample for that 10 you gave your dirt.

60 – 79: Swell. You are doing a good job in your garden. Gardening is a good hobby for you.

40 – 59: All right. You are in good company with most gardeners. You probably have some work to do to bring your garden up to a level that brings you more enjoyment. Don't we all? This is where the equation can help you improve your situation. Look across your ratings and see if you can move any of them up by switching out plants, buying better tools, adding more compost, or reducing chemical usage, for example.

20 – 39: Uh oh. I'm worried about you and your garden. Maybe you need to think about a good design to double your satisfaction with your plants, soil, and climate? Maybe you should move to a better gardening situation? What other numbers can you raise because I know that just by working through this equation, you want to enjoy your garden.

0 – 19: Sorry. I don't know what to say except maybe there is a better hobby for you other than gardening.

Have you considered stamp collecting or paint-by-number kits?

# CHAPTER 28

# TIME MANAGEMENT

In a pomodoro, I can get a lot done in the garden.

A pomodoro is 25 minutes, the unit of time used in a time management method known as the Pomodoro Technique. Francesco Cirillo, who came up with this time management method, used a tomato-shaped timer to keep track of his 25 minutes. The Italian word for tomato is *pomodoro*, hence he called the 25 minutes of time a pomodoro.

The idea is to spend 25 minutes, one pomodoro, on a task and then take a 5-minute break. Then move on to the next pomodoro either for a new task or the continuation of the first task. After four pomodoros, you can take a well-deserved 15- to 20-minute break.

This time management technique is especially useful when you are facing tasks you don't want to do, like weeding or turning compost. Instead of spending half the morning trying to motivate yourself to spend the morning weeding, you can tell yourself you just need to spend one pomodoro—25 minutes—weeding and then see how you feel. If you feel like weeding another 25 minutes after your 5-minute break, you can do that. Or you can move on to something else.

I have also found the Pomodoro Technique useful to remind myself when I'm kneeling in the garden, lost in thought while weeding a section of the garden, to get up every once in a while to stretch. Otherwise, I might not be able to get up at all when I've finished weeding.

I have also used a pomodoro timer on my smart phone to time some of my gardening tasks to convince myself they really don't take as long as I think they do. Believe it or not, there are multiple smart phone apps with tomato timers to help you keep track of your pomodoros. When I first used this technique, which admittedly I don't use every time I step out into the garden, I figured out it takes less than a pomodoro to mow my front lawn and just a little over a pomodoro to mow my back lawn if I walk fast.

Some gardeners might object to using time management in the garden. They don't want to feel rushed, constantly trying to beat the clock or the pomodoro timer. They just want to take their time and enjoy the experience. I wholeheartedly agree; they should do just that.

But I do use the pomodoro timer when I'm faced with a lot of weeding to do and need that extra bit of motivation to do it. Or when my time is limited. In those situations, I just start doing, taking a break every 25 minutes or so and a longer break after two hours. It has helped keep me more focused.

# CHAPTER 29

# TIME IN A GARDEN

It is true what the philosophers tell us: Time does stand still in a garden. This fact alone shapes how gardeners define time and their definitions are quite different than those used by people outside of the garden.

For non-gardeners, "just a minute" means about 60 seconds, give or take. However, a gardener will often use the phrase "just a minute" to describe the amount of time that it will take to do something simple in the garden that doesn't require them to change out of their street clothes into gardening togs. For example, a gardener might be walking out to their car to go to a movie and out of the corner of their eye, see a dead branch in the middle of an otherwise healthy shrub. They'll then holler out, "I'm going to go get the pruners and trim that branch out before we leave. It will take just a minute."

We know from observation that total elapsed time for just a minute in a garden is often as long as 30 minutes outside of the garden. This is often because when the gardener goes to get the pruners, the pruners aren't where they left them so they actually have to go looking for them. Once they find them, they see that a few container plantings need some water. There is no way they can watch a movie knowing their plants are suffering from lack of water. And since watering them will also take just a minute, they stop to do that too. While standing there watering the plant they look over to see a pretty bloom and accidentally water their shoes, which causes them to have to go back inside to put on another pair of shoes. No problem; it will take just a minute.

When they finally go back outside, they realize they left the pruners on the other side of the garden where they were watering the containers so they begin to walk back that way. It will take just a minute, stopping a few times to pull some weeds. Soon they have enough weeds in their hands that they decide to take them back to the compost bin on the edge of the vegetable garden. It will take just a minute. Once in the vegetable garden, they spot an almost perfect tomato, which of course they pick and take inside. It will take just a minute. Then they remember the dead branch and go back out front to cut it back. It will take just a minute, after all. It all took just a minute, and who cares about seeing all those movie previews anyway?

"Not long" is a fairly short amount of time to a non-gardener. Gardeners use the phrase "not long" to answer questions such as, "How long will that take?" For example, how long will it take to dig up that flowerbed? Not long. How long will it take to plant those bulbs? Not long. How long will it take to mow the lawn? Not long. What they really mean by "not long" is that they are willing to forsake housework, laundry, and other mundane activities to work in the garden. In fact, no matter where they are in the process of completing their latest project in the garden, the proper answer to any question about how long it will take, how long until it is finished, or how much longer they will be outside in the garden, is "not long."

How often are gardeners asked by someone outside the garden, "When are you going to stop gardening for the day?" The answer is, "In a bit." Gardeners use "in a bit" to indicate that at any time they will be finished in the garden and will come in. It could be in five minutes or it could be in five hours. It is most definitely in a bit. Really, given all that calls out for a gardener's attention in the garden, it is next to impossible to accurately predict when they will call it quits for the day, so they use the standard "in a bit."

Then there is "later." "Later" can be a confusing term for new gardeners because it doesn't actually describe time in a garden. It describes a timeframe outside of the garden. For example, when the sun is shining and the garden is too lovely to leave, the answer to any question about when a gardener is going to do something that doesn't involve gardening is "later." Later they will clean house or wash clothes or go pick up kids from school, because on nice days they all know that there is never enough time in the garden. There will be time later in winter to catch up on all the out-of-garden activities.

So go spend just a minute in the garden, then decide if you want to go inside in a bit. And if someone asks how long you plan to spend in the garden, just answer not long, and tell them you'll be in later.

# CHAPTER 30

 **and**

## DISTANCE IN A GARDEN

Gardeners speak their own language when describing distance in their gardens.

Planting instructions that dictate how far apart plants should be spaced might as well end with "or a little closer." That's because most gardeners tend to space their plants a little closer than the directions might indicate, if there are any directions. They set all the plants out where they think they should be and then decide a little closer is better. Or if a tag says to space the plants six to eight inches apart, six inches is better, or a little closer for good measure. In some cases, this achieves that fully planted look sooner. In other cases, this means that the plants get crowded out sooner, and some plants may have to be removed or trimmed back.

In a garden, "over there" is always where the tool is that the gardener wants. If they want someone else to go get that tool for them, it isn't really that far away. However, if the gardener has to stop what they are doing and go get that tool, it is quite a ways away from where they are tending their plants.

When a gardener decides there is a particular nursery, garden center, garden, or garden event they would like to visit, the distance to it magically becomes "not far." I would advise anyone who plans to go with a gardener on such a trip that is not far to make sure to go to the bathroom before they get in the car, pack some provisions including an overnight bag (just in case), check to see that the gas tank is full, and then relax and enjoy the drive. Though it's not far, it might be farther than they imagined and a few miles more.

"Not much" is how gardeners describe any type of garden bed or border expansion, especially if someone else wants to have a nice bit of lawn. "How much are you adding to that garden border?" "Not much," the gardener answers, as they proceed to slice out another foot width of sod, making the border five feet wide instead of the measly four feet wide it was before they decided to clean up the edge with a good sharp spade and add "not much" to the planting area.

And in the event someone figures out what all these distances really mean, gardeners can always revert to the universal "don't worry" as the answer to any questions anyone might ask about what they are doing in their gardens.

# CHAPTER 31

# QUANTITY IN A GARDEN

Quantities are relative, especially in a garden.

When gardeners say they want to get "a couple" fill-in-the-blank, as in "I think I'd like to get a couple loads of topsoil," this actually means that they would like to have upwards of eight loads of topsoil or some other quantity that is well more than two. By the way, two is generally not a number that most gardeners understand when buying anything gardening related, especially plants. Gardeners are always told to plant in threes, and two is never enough to do that.

When gardeners say "not too many" in response to someone asking them how many of something they bought, such as flats of annuals, this actually means that they bought one less than they really wanted to buy and more than any non-gardener could ever imagine, but they think they can handle the quantity they bought. The same applies to buying not too many seeds, not too many bulbs, not too many hoes, or not too many gardening magazines. Note "not many" is often used instead of "not too many" and is, in fact, often preferred because it implies a lesser quantity but may, in fact, be the same amount as "not too many." It's a subtle difference to keep in mind.

When gardeners say "a few" in reply to a question like, "How many bulbs did you buy?" they deliberately leave off a vital piece of information, the what, because a vague answer takes far less explaining than "a few dozen" or "a few hundred." So keep in mind that "a few" always refers to another larger quantity like a dozen, a hundred, or even a thousand.

Gardeners all know that "not as many as I wanted to get" generally refers to a quantity that most non-gardeners would not understand, so again, most gardeners make no attempt to explain it further. For example, when a gardener runs into a big sale at the garden center and there are seven plants available, they will want all seven but will just buy six, which is conveniently a multiple of three, which is the universally accepted minimum number of any one plant to buy. Then when asked how many they bought, the gardener's correct answer is "not as many as I wanted to get."

When gardeners say "a little" as in "I think I'll enlarge this flower bed just a little," it generally means they are going to double the size of it. And double the size often means to triple the size of it or increase the size of it until a barrier, like a property line, a fence, or the edge of someone's foot who thinks it is big enough, stops them. And if asked how big they are going to make a new flower bed or vegetable garden, most gardeners will reply with "not that big," which means that they are pretty sure they can dig it up themselves without renting a backhoe, but it is entirely possible that once they get started, they may have to get a backhoe to finish the job.

And yes, there are some advanced quantity definitions for gardeners, such as "a good start," which means they are never finished working on a garden, and "I didn't get them all" to imply how they generously left plants for others to buy at the local nursery. And when gardeners are really questioned about how many plants they purchased, there is always the universal, "Oh look, over there, isn't that an ice cream truck" or other suitable distraction.

CHAPTER 32

## SCREAMING AND CUSSING

Every gardener, at some point, should learn when it is appropriate to scream in the garden and when it is better to cuss.

First, let's address the scream. A scream, and by scream I mean one little "eh," not a blood-curdling scream that causes the neighbors to call the police, is only appropriate if you are startled or feel as though your life or that of your garden is in danger.

For example, if you are looking at a lovely flower border and see a vining plant where no vining plant should be, you should scream. Your garden is in danger! It is in danger of being overtaken by one of the most deadly of weeds, field bindweed. Once established in a garden, field bindweed is nearly impossible to eradicate.

After you scream, you need to take swift action to nip the vining plant literally in the bud. If you don't, well, I could scream just thinking about how awful it would be.

Other reasons to scream include if you see a big ugly spider, if a snake slithers across your path, or if someone accidentally dumps a truckload of cement on your front garden.

Please note the spider, snake, and cement examples are just that, examples. They did not happen to me.

So when is it appropriate to cuss in the garden? And by cuss, I mean only use the gardener's cuss word, frass, which is the fancy word for insect poop.

An example of an appropriate occasion to cuss is when you go out to your vegetable garden and see that the rabbits found your edamame plants—which you left unprotected—and ate them to nubbins. When that happens, you can certainly cuss with a well-stated "frass."

Other occasions for cussing include when you are weeding in a flower border and accidentally step on a tender new shoot just breaking through the ground or cut off a flower bud just as it was beginning to open. Or if you finish weeding and have just put your gloves and tools away and then spy a gigantic, thorny, nasty thistle hiding among the asters and you know you should pull it out immediately. Or if you find that some insect has chewed off most of the leaves of your columbine.

You get the idea. Scream when there is danger that might affect you or your garden. Cuss when you are annoyed. Follow these simple guidelines and you'll sound like the most experienced gardener in the neighborhood even if you just started gardening yesterday.

Then, once you've mastered screaming and cussing, learn to laugh and sing and whistle and hum in your garden because there is always a lot more good in a garden than bad.

# CHAPTER 33

## A GARDENER'S SPRINGTIME PLEDGE

Please raise your right hand and repeat after me:

I, *state your name*, am a gardener.

I pledge and promise that:

I will not panic if one week off work in the springtime is not enough time to complete all the projects I want to do in the garden.

I will faithfully weed in my garden so that at no time in summer will I have more weeds than flowers.

I will promptly plant any new plants within a few days of falling in love with them at the garden center, promising them a wonderful garden to grow in, and bringing them home.

I will water all my containers when needed, even if that is twice a day on the hottest summer days, remember to feed those contained, captive plants regularly, and make sure someone else will water them if I am gone.

I will mulch.

I will remain calm when the bugs arrive and begin devouring my garden. I will not resort to sprays or traps but will use safe methods to control them that don't harm the bees and other beneficial insects.

I will harvest everything from my vegetable garden

promptly and give extra produce to family, friends, and food banks.

I will not whine, complain, cry, or carry on (too much) if I don't get rain exactly when I think my garden needs it, or if the rain falls on the weekends, or otherwise interferes with my gardening activities.

I will not whine, complain, cry, or carry on (too much) if it gets too hot in summer.

I will prune as necessary to preserve the natural shape of a plant and never shape it into a nice round ball unless it is a boxwood.

I will deadhead rampant self-sowers promptly so they do not take over my garden.

I will share my knowledge of gardening with others along with passalong plants.

I will attempt to spend at least one-tenth of my time in the garden just sitting in it and enjoying it.

I will maintain my optimism throughout the growing season.

Having given this pledge and promise, I now step outside, ready for whatever my garden and Mother Nature send my way.

## CHAPTER 34

# SOME PEOPLE DON'T LIKE TO GARDEN

This may come as a shock to those who love to garden, but it appears that walking around on this planet are people who don't like to garden.

Breathe now. Clutch a few seed packets in your hand. Look out upon your garden full of flowers to center yourself. Then take a moment, if you must, to read that again, to reflect on what it means. Or skip on and forget you ever read this stunning bit of information.

I realize it is entirely possible that many gardeners already know this about people and actually accept and like—even love—people who don't like to garden. These people who don't like to garden could be in their families, in their neighborhoods, or at their places of work. They may pass them every day in the hallways at work or see them each morning at the local coffee shop and not know this about them. These people who don't like to garden look quite normal.

Many of these non-gardening people actually do like nice gardens and enjoy strolling down a garden path, admiring the flowers. But they often don't care one whit what the flowers are called or how they might grow them in their own gardens. Recently, some people have begun to refer to these non-gardeners as "plant blind." They don't see plants the same way gardeners see them. They see colors, they see green, but their interests don't go much beyond that.

Referring to the plants that might be around their house as "their own garden" might actually be a bit of a stretch. Truth be told, they probably paid good money to have others create a garden for them. But we all know that they are merely leasing that garden. To own a garden, you have to garden in it.

We also know that the fact these people don't like to garden does not make them bad people. They can be and often are people who contribute positively to society as a whole, just not by gardening.

Their reasons why they don't like to garden may seem irrational and trite to those of us who love to garden, or it may stem from some deeply rooted fears related to soil, plants, bugs, or an honest day's work in the hot sun.

Whatever their reasons for not gardening, it is not worth arguing with them about it. Nor is it worth trying to force them to garden. If you make them go out and work in a garden and then foolishly try to garden alongside them, you and they will both be miserable.

It is really for the best to let the non-gardener stay inside or sit quietly in a chair and watch as you, the gardener, happily and busily tend to the garden. Even if the work in the garden is hard and physically demanding, and it will sometimes be just that, keep a smile on your face, wear your best gardening hat and your special gardening shoes, and at all times make that non-gardener think they are missing out on the greatest experience of their life.

Because they are.

# CHAPTER 35

## A LETTER TO NEW VEGETABLE GARDENERS

*Dear New Vegetable Gardener,*

*Welcome to the world of gardening, new vegetable gardener. I am sure by now with a little success growing some flowers and maybe a few shrubs and a tree or two you are ready to grow some food. That's why I am writing to you. I am going to spill some beans on the principles of growing a little food for you and your family.*

*Principles, you ask? I know the word "principles" sounds highfalutin' and uppity-do-da-day. But bear with me and read my whole letter before you judge me and my principles. I hope you'll see that these principles are pretty simple, pretty easy, and pretty much intended to help guide any gardener to a life of happiness and good vegetables.*

Yes, I meant that—a life of happiness and good vegetables.

Once you know these principles you won't lose your mind reading seed catalogs, trying to decide what to grow. You won't fail miserably at growing vegetables. You won't give up hope during the hottest days of the summer. Put these five principles of vegetable gardening to work and you will soon be eating your own homegrown vegetables. I promise.

First and foremost, never reach for a chemical pesticide to solve a bug, weed, or disease problem in your vegetable garden. Commit to finding natural solutions for your bug, weed, or disease problems. I always tell people you can buy pesticide-laden vegetables at the grocery store, so grow your own vegetables using organic methods.

But you say you don't know how to use organic methods. Let me Google that for you! Within seconds you can do an online search about nearly any vegetable garden pest and find ways to control it without reaching for a spray, dust, or other chemical concoction. But do be careful of some of the scams and hocus-pocus methods that simply don't work and will make you look foolish. How do you know them when you see them? Use trusted sources like Cooperative Extension Service websites for your information.

Next, work at building up your soil. Add organic matter such as good compost and don't try to dig in the garden when the soil is wet. If you pay as much attention to building up the soil in the garden as you do tending the vegetables, your vegetables will practically grow themselves.

If you are not convinced that soil makes a difference,

go visit an experienced old-time vegetable gardener and look at their soil. I guarantee their soil will be rich with compost and look nothing like the gray subsoil left in your suburban garden after the builder scraped away the topsoil, or worse, deposited everything that was dug up for your basement on top of your good topsoil.

Once you've committed to organic growing in good soil, grow what you like to eat. There is no sense growing vegetables you aren't going to eat. You might as well grow flowers. But remember that what you like to eat will change when you grow the vegetables yourself. So please, even if you don't like a particular vegetable, commit to growing it at least once and trying it again. You may find you like that once-yucky vegetable when you grow it yourself.

Over time, you'll figure out your tried-and-true varieties of vegetables to grow. I recommend you grow those each year, but also try at least one new variety of a vegetable you love and one new vegetable that you don't think you like. One of the new vegetables may be your greatest triumph of the growing season and earn a place on your "tried-and-true" list.

Please also remember to make the garden only as large as you think you can tend on your own. Generally in most families it falls to one person to care for the vegetable garden, so don't make the garden so large that it gets away from you by midsummer and becomes a big weedy mess.

And even if the garden becomes a big weedy mess by midsummer don't give up on it. Spend a morning or two bringing it back by weeding it and pulling out spent plants, those that aren't producing any longer. You'll be surprised *how the vegetable plants that are left will respond and grow and produce for you.*

*Finally, don't fuss and worry about what could go wrong in the garden. Remember what can go right. So what if your spacing is a little off or you are a week or two late in planting? Or you don't pull every weed? Fortunately, a vegetable garden doesn't require perfection to produce food so you'll still get some good food for your efforts, whatever they are.*

*Dear new vegetable gardener, because I am impressed by your enthusiasm and want you to be successful growing whatever vegetables you want to grow, here's a bonus sixth principle for growing vegetables.*

*Visit your garden daily. The more time you spend in your garden—even if it is just five minutes early in the morning or right before the sun sets—the more you learn about it. You can catch problems early on before they take hold and destroy an entire crop. And more importantly, you can harvest vegetables at their peak and enjoy some of the best food you've ever eaten.*

*Trust me. Adopt these principles of vegetable gardening, and you'll enjoy a life of happiness and good vegetables.*

*With a shared love of gardening,*
*Carol*

# CHAPTER 36

## GARDEN IT FORWARD

We must be ready at a moment's notice to reach out to the Great Ungardened.

We must recognize when there is a spark of interest in gardening and growing plants in the Great Ungardened so that we are ready with an idea or thought that will turn that spark into a burning desire to go outside and plant something.

We must be ready to lend a hand or a tool or a seed or a plant to the Great Ungardened, to garden it forward so they, too, can become gardeners.

What is this "garden it forward" all about? A nearly forgotten southern writer, Lily Hardy Hammonds, is credited with first writing the now popular phrase "pay it forward." She included it in a book she wrote in 1916, *In the Garden of Delights*, which really isn't about gardening but is a memoir. She wrote in that book, "You don't pay love back, you pay it forward."

Love, gardening, it's all the same to a gardener, right? Well, not really, but the point is, you don't pay another gardener back for helping you learn to garden. You pay it back—you garden it forward—by helping someone else become a gardener too.

We must be ready to garden it forward when the opportunity is there.

We must become gardenangelists, evangelists for gardening.

I am ready when someone mentions to me that they are thinking about planting a vegetable garden. I know without a moment's hesitation what simple advice to share on how to plant a first vegetable garden in just a few hours. I know which vegetables are easy to grow and provide great harvests in my area.

I am ready to share the secrets to happiness in the garden when someone mentions an interest in doing more in their garden than planting a row of evergreen shrubs across the front of their house.

In the springtime, especially, even the Great Ungardened will look around as flowers begin to bloom about them and think, perhaps just for a minute, that they might enjoy a lovely garden, might find some benefit for their family if not themselves in growing a few vegetables. We must recognize those moments and be ready with advice and assurance that they, too, can become a gardener.

We must be gardenangelists who garden it forward.

# ACKNOWLEDGEMENTS

Writing this book has been like opening seed packets and sowing the seeds they contain to see what will grow. The essays I've included were once packets of bits and bytes living in an online world on my blog *maydreamsgardens.com*. With this book, I've opened those packets and put the words and essays onto paper.

I have many people to acknowledge and thank— many good friends who encouraged me along the way. Some of them actually took up their own pens to help shape this final book. Thank you, Deb Wiley, for working with me on early drafts of my book, providing valued editorial input and encouragement. Thank you, Dee Nash, Mary Ann Newcomer, and Jo Ellen Meyers Sharp for encouraging me through the years.

I am also grateful to Katie Elzer-Peters from the *thegardenofwords.com* and her team of Billie Brownell and Nathan Bauer who helped bring this book to life.

I would also like to thank the many fellow gardeners—and one non-gardener, my mom— who over the years read my blog posts and magazine articles and encouraged me with their comments and accolades. The list is long but I'd like to especially thank Cindy, Frances, Gail, Kathy, Layanee, Leslie, and Robin.

I'm indebted, too, to GWA: The Association of Garden Communicators whose members welcomed me, encouraged me, and validated me.

Thank you also to my sisters, Kathy, Karen, and Sherry, who have always supported me as a gardener and writer.

For those holding this book in your hands, there are words embedded in the graphics at the beginning of each chapter. These graphics originally came from *The Garden's Story* by George H. Ellwanger (D. Appleton and Co., 1889), a book I found on one of my frequent trips to a used book store. Nathan Bauer from *thegardenofwords.com* embedded the words at my request. If you put all those words together in chapter order you'll discover my five secrets for achieving happiness in your garden.

If by chance you bought your copy of this book directly from me, you may also discover a note, a bookmark, or perhaps a seed packet slipped between two of the pages, reminiscent of some of the treasures I've found in old gardening books, placed there by previous owners long before I discovered them.

Finally, thank you for purchasing this book. I hope you find these essays enjoyable, especially if, like me, you live the gardening life with humor and a sense of play and fun.

## ABOUT THE AUTHOR

Carol Michel is a lifelong gardener and resident of Indiana with a Bachelor's degree in Horticulture Production from Purdue University. She spent over three decades making a living working in healthcare IT while making a life for herself in her garden. Now she calls herself a "gardenangelist" and spends most of her time in her garden, sharing all things gardening with anyone who will listen. She is an avid collector of old gardening books and claims to have the largest hoe collection in the world. She regularly writes about her old books, hoes, and many other gardening related topics for Indiana Gardening and her award-winning garden blog, www.maydreamsgardens.com.

# LOOKING FOR A LITTLE MORE INFORMATION?

I continue to post to my blog *maydreamsgardens.com* and encourage you to subscribe to it so you don't miss a single post.

Like many gardeners and authors, you can also find me on several social media outlets.

Currently, I have two pages on Facebook:

- May Dreams Gardens, where you will find information about my gardening exploits.

- Gardenangelist, where I share gardening information I've found around the internet.

I am @Indygardener on Twitter, where I tweet about gardening and life, and on Instagram, where I mostly post pretty pictures of flowers and gardens.

If you are interested in getting involved with other garden writers, please check out GWA: The Association of Garden Communicators, gardenwriters.org.

If you think you would like to publish your own book, I recommend thegardenofwords.com as a place to start your search for assistance.

If you are interested in meeting other gardeners in your local area, join or start a garden club. Hang out at the local garden centers and greenhouses. Enroll in a Master Gardeners class offered by your local cooperative extension service. Start your own blog and tell the world about your garden. Just don't stay behind your garden gate, gardening alone.

And if you just want to ask me something, feel free to email me at indygardener@gmail.com.

90456421R00080

Made in the USA
Columbia, SC
04 March 2018